The Battle of New Orleans

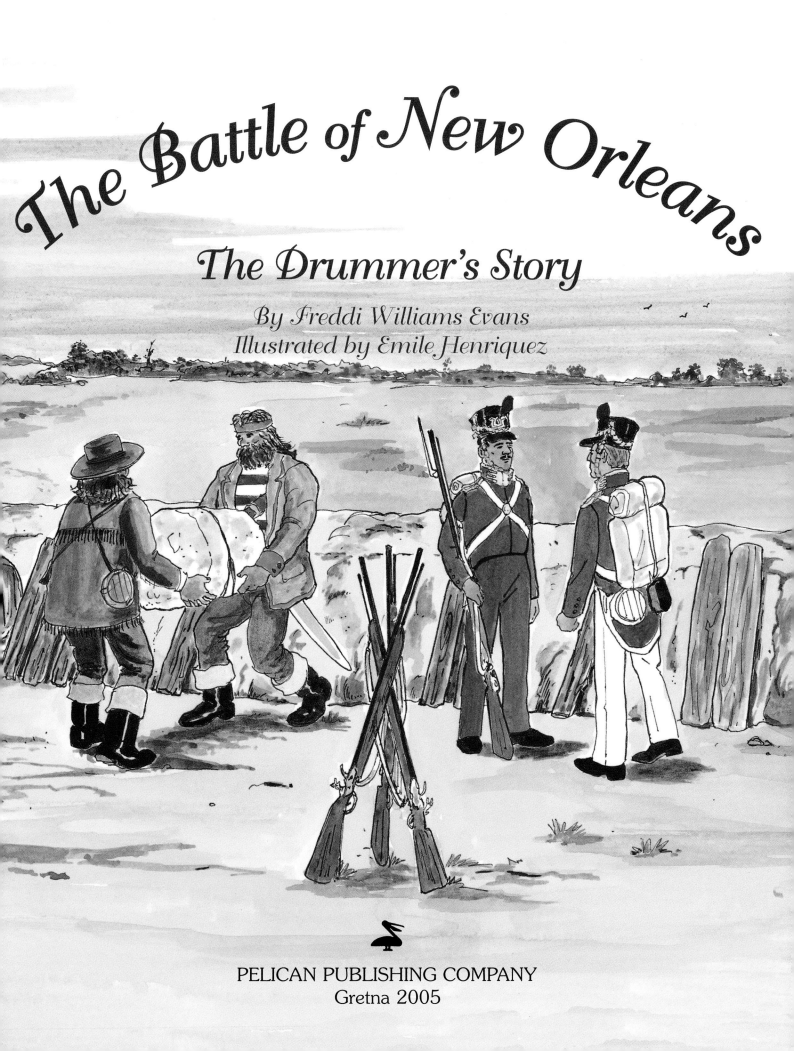

The Battle of New Orleans

The Drummer's Story

By Freddi Williams Evans

Illustrated by Emile Henriquez

PELICAN PUBLISHING COMPANY
Gretna 2005

To my grandparents: Ed and Geraldine Cotten;
Fannie Williams Sanders, Perry Williams,
and Phil Sanders

Library of Congress
Cataloging-in-Publication Data

Evans, Freddi Williams.
  The Battle of New Orleans : the drummer's story / by
Freddi Williams Evans ; illustrated by Emile
Henriquez.
      p. cm.
  Summary: "Old Jordan" tells how, when he was a boy,
he used his drum to summon General Andrew
Jackson's troops into action in the 1815 Battle of New
Orleans.
  ISBN-13: 978-1-58980-300-8 (alk. paper)
  [1. Drummers (Musicians)—Fiction. 2. New Orleans,
Battle of, New Orleans, La., 1815—Fiction. 3. Stories
in rhyme.] I. Henriquez, Emile F., ill. II. Title.

  PZ8.3.E89933Bat 2005
  [E]—dc22
                                    2004031085

Printed in Singapore
Published by Pelican Publishing Company, Inc.
1000 Burmaster Street, Gretna, Louisiana 70053

THE BATTLE OF NEW ORLEANS:
THE DRUMMER'S STORY

Rat-ti-ty tat, rat-ti-ty tat tat went the drum's beat
As the gray-haired drummer marched down the street.

"Old Jordan, Old Jordan," his name rang in the air.
He was the crowd's favorite; no one could compare.

Jordan played long drum rolls and different kinds of drills.
He played snazzy, snappy beats that gave the crowd thrills.
People clapped and cheered as he marched along—
Stepping to the sound of an old war song.

Other gray-haired men followed closely behind
Wearing faded uniforms of all different kinds.

The soldiers waved flags as they passed by,
Marching to the beat of the drum's war cry.

I followed Old Jordan as he marched down the street.
I pretended I had his drum and made it sound just as sweet.

Rat-ti-ty tat, rat-ti-ty tat tat, did-dle, did-dle, dee—
If I really had his drum, a *great* drummer I would be.

Then the parade ended, and Old Jordan sat to rest.
So I dashed to his side to make a big request.

"May I beat your drum, Mister Jordan? I like the way it sounds.
I like the way it rattle-tattles when you play it through the town."

"Well, this is a special drum, and I play it a special way.
I play it the way I played it on the battlefield that day.

"The British were trying to take New Orleans, but we
    were ready for their attack.
Nearly four thousand men lined up, just waiting to
    fight back.

"There were French, Spanish, German, and men of
   color, enslaved and free,
Kentucky riflemen, Mississippi dragoons, and
   sharpshooters from Tennessee.

"Jean Lafitte and his pirates, Cajuns, Indians, and
   men from Haiti
All stood side by side, to fight for freedom and liberty.

"We built breastwork a mile long across that
   Chalmette field.
Dirt, logs, wooden kegs, and cotton bales served
   as our shield.

"The Jackson Line we called it—after our general,
   Andrew Jackson, you see.
The line spread from the river to the swamp—gunboats,
   muskets, and artillery.

"The redcoats tried to surprise us, just before the break of dawn.
We saw their shadows in the fog. Someone fired, and the battle
    was on.
I beat this drum fast. I beat it with all my might.
I beat it to give the soldiers spirit. I beat it to tell them to fight.

"I beat my drum loud—loud as the ones at Congo
  Square.
Grapeshot, bullets, and cannonballs blasted through
  the air.

"The general yelled, 'Give it to them, boys; let's finish the business today!'
Then I beat the reveille so loud, the whole battlefield could hear me play.

"I played from beginning to end—never put down this drum of mine.
I had to keep the soldiers fighting when they were on the line.

"Yes, I played till it was over, till the British were
     running back.
It took around thirty minutes from the time they
     made their attack.

"General Jackson shook my hand for a job well done. We all celebrated. The Battle of New Orleans had been won.

That was January 8, 1815, but my job was not complete. There were more battles to fight and more enemies to defeat."

The sun kissed the drummer's copper-toned face
As he told about war with pride and with grace.

Then the old man stood to go on his way—
To continue celebrating January 8th Day.

But suddenly, Old Jordan stopped and beckoned my way.
My heart beat like the drum. It was my turn to play.
He placed the drum by my leg and swung the strap over
　my head.
He slid the sticks between my fingers. "Tell the soldiers to
　fight," he said.

Rat-tat tat, rat-tat tat. I gripped the sticks and started to play.

"Redcoats are coming," Old Jordan yelled. "Finish the job today!"

Rat-ty tat tat. I played faster—my left hand, then my right.

Rat-ty tat tat. "That's it!" he said. "That helps the soldiers fight."

Rat-ty tat tat. I beat the drum loud—loud as Old Jordan did.
Rat-ty tat tat. "That's it!" he cheered. "That's good playing, kid."

Then I played Old Jordan's drum as we marched down
the street—
The gray-haired drummer and me, marching to my new
drumbeat.

GLOSSARY

artillery—weapons used in war, especially cannons

breastwork—a barrier or wall behind which soldiers stood for protection

Congo Square—the public square located on Rampart Street in New Orleans where enslaved Africans and free people of color gathered on Sunday afternoons to play musical instruments, sing, and dance

cotton bales—large bundles of cotton

dragoons—armed fighters on horseback

grapeshot—a cluster of small cast-iron balls shot from a cannon

redcoats—a name given to the British because of the color of their uniforms

reveille—a drum or bugle signal that alerted soldiers to action

sharpshooters—fighters who shoot with great accuracy